CALANAIS
The Standing Stones

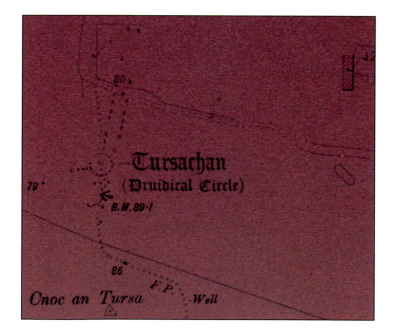

The publishers acknowledge financial assistance towards this publication
from the following: Historic Scotland, Western Isles Enterprise
Western Isles Islands Council, Scottish Natural Heritage,
Western Isles Tourist Board, Western Isles, Skye and Lochalsh LEADER.

The author gratefully acknowledges the following:

Mr and Mrs MacArthur of Breasclete, for their hospitality, Mrs Mackenzie of
Calanais, who took care of our children, and the staff of Breasclete School
who educated them while we excavated.

All those who took part in the excavation: Mr Angus Morrison, and
Carloway Estate, who allowed us to excavate east of the area which was then
in the care of the State.

Gerald Ponting, Margaret Ponting (Curtis) and Ron Curtis, with whom it has,
over the last two decades, been a pleasure to discuss, Calanais.

Historic Scotland and, in particular (in alphabetical order) Ian Armit, Mike
Brooks, Noel Fojut, Duncan Macniven and Joe White, for their support and
help.

Simon Fraser and Susan Maclennan for advice and suggestions throughout
the writing of this book, Fionna Ashmore, Noel Fojut and Anna and Graham
Ritchie for comments on an earlier draft. I am particularly grateful to Heather
Delday of Acair for close collaboration on the design.

First published in Scotland in 1995 by Urras nan Tursachan Ltd
© 1995 Urras nan Tursachan Ltd
© Patrick Ashmore

Design and typesetting by Acair Ltd, Stornoway, Isle of Lewis
Printed by Highland Printers, Inverness

ISBN 0 86152 161 7

Photography

Historic Scotland:
Title page ,10, 16, 30, 33, 34, 35, 51
8 (Trevor Cowie)
17, 18, 37, 41, 42 (Mike Brooks)
27, 31, 50, 33 (Patrick Ashmore)

The Royal Commission on the Ancient and Historical
Monuments of Scotland: Inside front and back covers, 11, 14, 23, 25.
Science Photo Library, Simon Fraser: 7.
National Museums of Scotland: 9.
Margaret and Ron Curtis: 40.
Raymond Lamb, (Orkney Heritage Society): 10.
George Wyllie: 18.
John MacKinnon: 38.
Charles Tait: 5, 8, 30.
Colin Ruscoe: 45.
Duncan Morison: 19.
James Smith: 34, 49, 50.
Colin Ruscoe: 45.
Nationalmuseet, Copenhagen: 17, 21.
A Description of the Western Isles of Scotland,
Martin Martin. First published 1703.
Proceedings of the Society of Antiquaries of Scotland. Vol III,
Stornoway Public Library.
Saint Andrews University: 24, 25.
George Washington Wilson, Stornoway Public Library: 26.

Illustration

Dave Pollock: 30, 31, 32, 33, 36.
Owen Butler: 6, 12, 15, 28, 32, 39.
Alan Braby: 9.
Michael Leybourne: 51.

Illuminating the stones: Sam Maynard, Eric Hoffmann,
Will Maclean, Reinhard Behrens, John Morisone, George Wyllie,
Marius Alexander, Iain Crichton Smith, Derick Thomson,
Murdo MacLeod, Gus Wylie.

Cover photograph: John MacKinnon/Eòlas.

Contents

Foreword

I have always known it as Callanish, or even Callernish. Before that it was called Classerniss. Now we must get used to calling it Calanais, the original Gaelic form of the name which will be enshrined in the next Ordnance Survey maps of the Western Isles. And a good thing, too.

More and more we are coming to recognise that the past, however distant, is of profound relevance to our present and to our future. Over the millennia, human cultural activity has always depended on the natural environment. Indeed it is this intimate interaction which has created the landscape of the Scotland we have inherited and which continues to evolve to create the inheritance of future generations.

It is this combination of natural and cultural heritage which people all over the world find so alluring, and which the people of the Western Isles are now celebrating with such verve.

As this is written, a major exhibition of the arts related to Calanais is running in Stornoway. 1995 has been designated as the Year of Archaeology. And the splendid new Visitor Centre at Calanais will enable residents and visitors alike to appreciate to the full the remarkable experience of Calanais without causing damage to the marvellous heirloom they have come to admire and to enjoy.

This excellent book will explain, and inform, and stimulate. And that's a good thing, too.

Magnus Magnusson KBE

1 Calanais – a centre of power

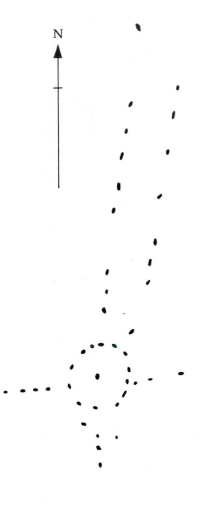

N

The main stone setting at Calanais is an extraordinary monument, an ancient centre of power. Within a few kilometres of it are many other ritual sites. Why were they built here?

Well, the climate was warmer and the sea-level was lower. Peat had not started to blanket the land. Barley could be grown on the broad ridge where Calanais stands, and elsewhere. The hills provided rough grazing for red deer, sheep and cattle. In those valleys sheltered from the winds grew scrub and woodland. Where the tides now cover the land there were probably grasslands, and marshes full of seasonal bird life. Salmon ran in the rivers, and the sea was full of fish and shell fish. The land and sea could support many people.

Perhaps the building of Calanais gave people a purpose in common, allowing stability even during a period of change when growing populations demanded new forms of society. Elsewhere, around 3000 BC. (5000 years ago), a cult or religion, involving the building of large earthen enclosures and the setting up of tall stones and timber circles, seems to have swept through Britain. Sunrise and sunset at midwinter seem to have been indicated by the direction of the entrance passages of great tombs.

The most attractive explanation for the building of the stone settings in this area is that every 18.6 years, the moon skims especially low over the southern hills. It seems to dance along them, like a great god visiting the earth. Knowledge and prediction of this heavenly event gave earthly authority to those who watched the skies. At Calanais, this power was given material expression by a people for whom the cycles of the sea, of their lives and of the heavens provided the foundations for a rich set of beliefs.

2 People in the ancient landscape

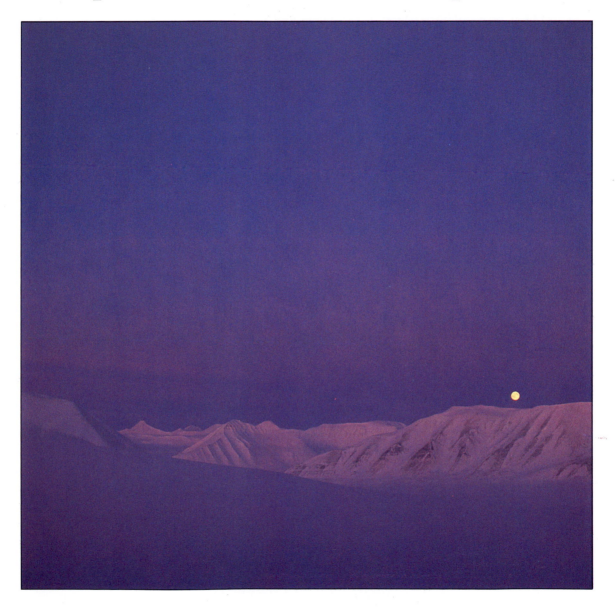

During the last glaciation the sky sucked up the sea, whose waters fell as snow. Scotland was covered by an ice mass. Ocean levels dropped well below those of today, revealing land which is now below water. After 13,500 BC, the offshore plains of west Lewis were deluged as the world warmed up. Through all the time people have lived on Lewis the sea has been slowly rising. Even 3500 years ago, when these Bronze Age walls were built, there was dry land with pastures, arable fields and birch, willow, rowan and hazel woods where now the tide ebbs and flows in the inlets of Loch Roag.

These bronze age walls discovered near Calanais during peat-cutting, are part of a field system that runs below high water mark

The first arable fields around Calanais were cultivated before 4000 BC. Barley – bere or bear is the everyday name for this primitive variety – was probably the main crop. Farming on the rigs (narrow earthen ridges created for seed beds) under the Standing Stones probably started many centuries later. Ten to twenty generations before the Standing Stones were set up, the rigs were abandoned and covered by grass and heather, while birches spread over the fields in the valleys around.

Tree stumps preserved in the peat

Discoveries elsewhere in the Western Isles help us understand what we may find around Calanais, surviving from the period when the rigs were in use. This settlement at Loch Olabhat in North Uist was built on a small island. It seems to have contained only one house at any one time. The pottery used in the settlement was of a Western Isles type which was found in small amounts at Calanais. There were probably similar houses somewhere close to where the Standing Stones were later erected.

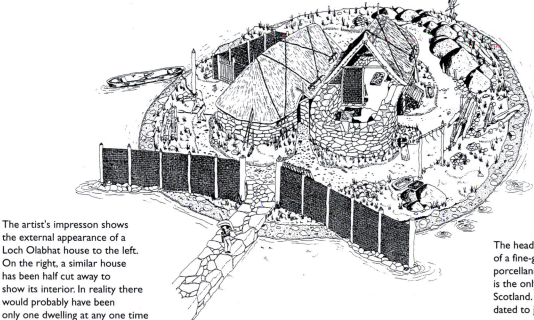

The artist's impresson shows the external appearance of a Loch Olabhat house to the left. On the right, a similar house has been half cut away to show its interior. In reality there would probably have been only one dwelling at any one time

The head of this axe was made of a fine-grained stone called porcellanite. The finely carved haft is the only known example from Scotland. It has been radiocarbon dated to just before 3000 BC

Around 3200 to 3000 BC this fine stone axe was lost or hidden in peat at Shulishader, near Stornoway. It was a prestige object, a sign of a growing elite in Lewis, for the axe-head was probably imported from Antrim. The wealth of that elite was supported by small scale agriculture, which flourished in the area, but its control of the people was probably based on links with distant places and beliefs about the movements of the sun and moon.

Around 3000 BC, when the Standing Stones were erected, great changes were taking place throughout Britain. It was the beginning of the end of the building of chambered tombs, although paradoxically some of the finest were created around that time. As new ideas spread, earthen enclosures with massive banks and ditches were laboriously constructed, and timber and tall stone circles were set up inside them. The people lived in small settlements containing several houses.

Part of the reconstructed settlement at Barnhouse, Orkney. This exceptionally large building was probably designed for ceremonial purposes.

There is an intriguing possibility that there was, near Calanais, a settlement like this one at Barnhouse in the Orkney islands. Barnhouse is of much the same date as the tall stone circle 250 metres away at Stenness and very similar pottery was used at both sites – pottery called grooved ware, which was also used at the stone circle at Calanais. So perhaps a settlement of straight-sided, round cornered houses, containing square hearths and with built-in beds, is waiting to be discovered beneath the peat or the lazy beds of Calanais.

About 2600 to 2500 BC, stock farming became more important locally. One of the mysteries of Calanais is whether the small chambered cairn inside the ring was built at the heart of a flourishing agricultural community, or on marginal pastures at a time when the focus of settlement had moved away.

The Stones of Stenness, Orkney. Structures like those within the building shown above were found during excavation inside this stone circle

3 The sites around Calanais

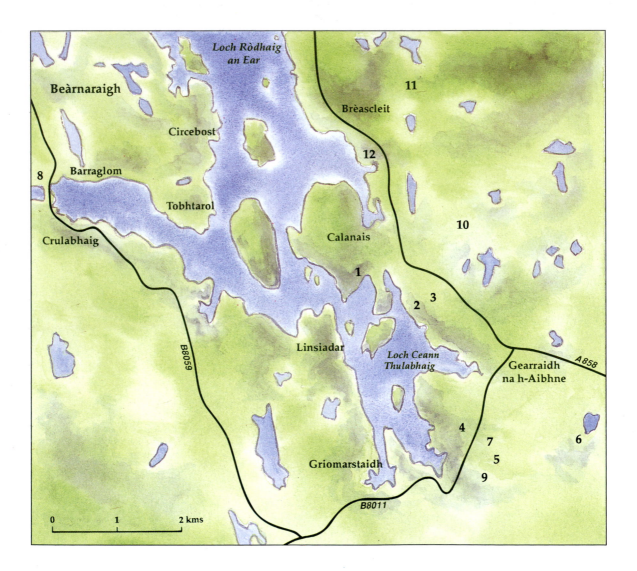

Site 1   Calanais

Site 2   Cnoc Ceann a' Ghàrraidh

Site 3   Cnoc Fhillibhir Bheag

Site 4   Ceann Thulabhaig

Site 5   Airigh nam Bidearan

Site 6   Cùl a' Chleit

Site 7   Cnoc Dubh

Site 8   Airigh Mhaoldonaich

Site 9   Druim nam Bidearan

Site 10   Na Dromannan

Site 11   Airigh na Beinne Bige

Site 12   Stonefield

Site	Name	Brief Description	Other names
1	**Calanais** *(pronounced approx. Kalanish)*	The main site, a cross-shaped setting, centred on a ring of stones containing a central monolith and a small chambered cairn.	Classerniss; Callernish; Callanish; Tursachan Callernish; The Standing Stones of Callanish; Callanish I
2	**Cnoc Ceann a' Ghàrraidh** *(pronounced approx. krok kyain a gaa-ree - this is not a mistake: 'cn' is indeed (pronounced approximately 'kr')*	A stone ring; 5 standing stones and 3 fallen ones lie on its circuit. When it was cleared of peat in 1858 a fallen stone, a rough cairn, and sockets for timber uprights were found inside it.	*hillock at the end of the wall;* Knock Ceann a Gharie; Cnoc Ceann; Loch Roag; Cnoc Ceann a'Gharaidh; Callanish II
3	**Cnoc Fillibhir Bheag** *pronounced approx. kroc fill-i-ver veg)*	A stone ring with 8 stones standing on its circuit and 4 inside it. Several fallen stones were discovered when it was cleared of peat in 1858.	*little fillibhir hillock;* Knock Mhelivir; Cnoc Fillibhir; Callanish III
4	**Ceann Thulabhaig** *(pronounced approx. kyain hoo-la-vig)*	A stone ring with 5 standing stones and a fallen stone. A small central cairn includes a little standing stone.	*head of Hula bay;* Ceann Hulivig; Ceann Hulavig; Cean Thulabig Tursachan Ceann Thulabhig Ceann Thulabeg; Garynahine; Loch Roag; Callanish IV
5	**Airigh nam Bidearan** *(pronounced approx. aa-ree nam bidge-ya-ran)*	The most prominent remains are 3 standing stones in a row, which may be part of a field system or have been designed to point to the most northerly moon-set.	*shieling of the pinnacles;* Airidh nam Bideran; Tursachan Airidh nam Bidearan;; Callanish V
6	**Cùl a' Chleit** *(pronounced approx. kool a hletch)*	Most of this is a relatively recent abandoned settlement; 2 standing stones may be part of it, or part of a prehistoric cairn or stone setting.	*rocky cliff at the back;* Cul a' Chleit; Callanish VI
7	**Cnoc Dubh** *(pronounced approx. kroc doo)*	A relatively recent ruined house, which has been thought by some people to be an ancient site.	*black hillock;* Chnoc Dhubh; Cnoc a botha; Callanish VII
8	**Cleitir** *(pronounced approx. kletch-er)*	Four standing stones, set in a deliberately levelled area on the cliff overlooking the sea channel separating Great Bernera from mainland Lewis. What may be a fallen standing stone, at Airigh Mhaoldonaich, lies on a direct line between this site and Site 11.	*cliffs;* "Tursachan" Barraglom; Great Bernera(y); Bernera Bridge; Cleiter; Callanish VIII
9	**Druim nam Bidearan** *(pronounced approx. drym nam bidge-ya-ran)*	Two fallen stones next to what may be the holes in which they stood.	*ridge of the pinnacles;* Druim nan Bidearan; Callanish IX
10	**Na Dromannan** *(pronounced approx. na drom-an-an)*	11 large stones which probably represent a fallen stone circle. A steep rock face nearby allows easy quarrying of large slabs.	*the ridges or the backs;* Druim nan Eum (in error); Druim nan Eun (in error); Callanish X
11	**Airigh na Beinne Bige** *(prounounced approx. aa-ree na bain-ye beg)*	A single standing stone. It may have been part of a larger setting.	*shieling of the little hill;* Callanish XI
12	**Stonefield** *(pronounced approx. Stone-field)*	A stone discovered in 1923. It stands at its original position	Blair; Callanish XII

The table is a modified version of that in Gerald and Margaret Ponting's Callanish: the documentary records; Part 2: the minor sites (Callanish 1981). They collected the names with the help of John MacIver of Breasclete. The names were checked by Donald MacAulay, a native of Great Bernera, now Professor of Celtic Studies at Glasgow University. This numbering of the sites started with Professor Alexander Thom and has since been extended by others.

The Main Setting (Site 1)

The bold pattern of 19th century farming dominates the air photograph on the opposite page, articulating the land. In the middle of the agricultural lazy beds there is a gap, revealing a land surface resurrected from beneath a 5 feet deep blanket of peat. Into that surface are set the great stones of Calanais.

The stone ring is not a true circle, and it is not certain how it was laid out. It is symmetrical, set along a line running true east-west through the centre of the huge central stone. The western half of the ring is a true semi-circle, but the eastern half is flattened, as if the ring faced the spring sunrise. The southern row runs nearly due south towards the natural outcrop called Cnoc an Tursa. However, the south row is not really straight and the stones of the ring are not precisely on any neat geometrical figure. The sense we impose on them is a modern sense, not necessarily a rediscovery of an ancient meaning.

The eastern row consists of five stones. It is crooked but it points generally somewhat north of due east. The western row does seem straighter. By chance it points pretty accurately along the Ordnance Survey gridlines plotted on modern maps, which should warn us not to make too much of seemingly significant alignments.

The avenue is broader in the north, narrowing as it approaches the circle. Some stones have been lost and the traces of agricultural lazy beds north of the modern track crossing the avenue suggest they were uprooted during agriculture. Its east side is nearly straight. The west side has a kink in it: the three stones nearest the circle form a row pointing to the central monolith, while the rest are roughly parallel to the eastern side. Perhaps the avenue was used for ceremonial approaches to the circle, but it may have had a different purpose, related to the movements of the moon.

Inside the stone ring is a small chambered tomb. Just to the east are traces of a later structure.

N

The satellite sites

Cnoc Ceann a' Ghàrraidh (Site 2) is the closest to the main site. It has five standing stones between 2.4 and 3.5 metres tall, and at least two fallen stones, forming an oval stone ring. When it was cleared of peat, shortly after the main site, at least five small holes lined with pebbles from the seashore were discovered in its interior. Bits of charcoal were found in the holes, which may have held wooden uprights. Small sites like this seem to have been used throughout early prehistory for cremation burials and other rituals, so it is very difficult to say what relationship Cnoc Ceann a' Ghàrraidh bore to the main site, although it is generally supposed that it and the other satellite circles were later.

Cnoc Fhillibhir Bheag (Site 3) consists of twelve stones up to three metres tall set in an apparently haphazard pattern. It has been interpreted in two main ways; either as two rough ellipses, one inside the other, or as a ring with a flattened side (like the ring at the main site) with four stones set up inside it. Some of the original stones are perhaps missing, and probably the stones represent more than one phase of building.

Ceann Thulabhaig (Site 4) was sketched by J J A Worsaae in 1846, before it was cleared of peat. The five standing stones are the remains of an oval ring and are up to 2.7 metres tall. Inside the ring is a low, rough cairn which now includes one small upright central stone.

The tall stones at Sites 1-4 are their most prominent feature. Enough is visible at them to suggest long histories in which the standing stones only played one part. Other sites are not so obvious; to an even greater extent their nature is concealed.

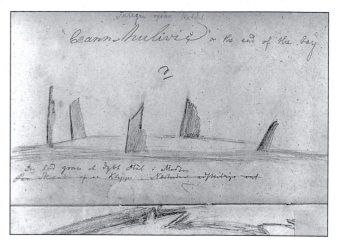

Close to what seems to be a destroyed stone circle on **Na Dromannan** (Site 10), about 1.5 km from the main site, a cliff provides abundant natural rough slabs, and it has been suggested that this was the source of the standing stones. Massive though they seem, most of them can be moved quite easily by a few people using wooden rollers. Only the larger ones would require the combined efforts of many families.

There are many other sites nearby. Not all of the twelve shown on the map are ancient (See page 13), but they include the remains of burial cairns, alignments and other prehistoric structures. Look at the landscape, and think of between 150 and 200 generations of continuous farming and worship before Christ was born.

The Lewisian gneiss was formed long before life began. It was the bedrock of the oldest land surface so far recognised in Britain. Its composition and appearance today show the effects of great heat and pressure

18

4 The main site – antiquaries and owners

Sir James Matheson, owned Lewis at the time the Standing Stones were cleared of peat. His wife, Lady Matheson, inherited Lewis after her husband's death

The first plan of Calanais, engraved for Martin Martin and published in 1703

In the 17th century the people of Lewis called standing stones Fir Bhrèige – false men – and around 1680 John Morisone wrote that *It is left by traditione that these were a sort of men converted into stone by ane Inchanter. others affirme that they were sett up in places for devotione.* Martin Martin, who visited Calanais about 1695, was probably influenced by mainland ideas when he reported that *... they told me, it was a Place appointed for Worship in the time of Heathenism, and that the Chief Druid or Priest stood near the big Stone in the centre, from whence he address'd himself to the People that surrounded him.*

Martin Martin's account was very popular. No doubt that was partly because antiquarians were besotted by the idea of Druids – some believing them to be the presiding geniuses of a golden age, others that they demanded cruel sacrifices. However, another attraction was the plan he provided. Here was grist to the mill of learned fancy: an ounce of inspiration allied to a grain of perspiration brought forth plenty of explanations. To some the twelve stones of Martin Martin's circle stood for the signs of the zodiac, the rows symbolised the four principal winds, and the nineteen stones which Martin Martin claimed stood on either side of the avenue represented the solar cycle. In 1743 William Stukely, the most famous antiquarian of the age, twisting the avenue to his own purposes, explained it as a Druidical circle and serpent. Many other fantastical ideas were published, based on bookish studies which added little or nothing to our knowledge of the site.

The first reasonably accurate description of Calanais was written by a geologist, John MacCulloch, in 1819. He depicted the setting as a rectilinear cross and got details wrong, but we can deduce that, apart from some stones which have disappeared from the avenue and the removal of 5ft of peat, the setting was much as we see it today.

In 1846 the illustrious Danish prehistorian, J J A Worsaae visited Calanais. He was 25 years old and he was fulfilling the recommendation he had made in his important book 'Danmarks Oldtid'; *In order that the Danish memorials may appear in their true light and connection, it will be important to enquire in what regions of other countries ... monuments of antiquity have been observed ...*

Worsaae drew this sketch plan of the circle. Like MacCulloch he showed five stones in the west row (only four are known) and his marginal notes suggest there were five visible in the east row. His delightful sketch, reproduced below shows the stones of the circle in deep peat. North of the circle the peat had been cut away, although not cleared entirely; and while the peat dropped away sharply on the east side, to the west it seems to have remained uncut.

Worsaae's plan of 1846

Meanwhile, sad to record, there had been little progress in thinking amongst some antiquarians. Perhaps the new ideas publicised by Worsaae, of a Stone Age followed by Bronze and Iron Ages, were too much to take in. In 1854 Callender published a paper about Calanais in the Proceedings of the Society of Antiquaries of Scotland, in which stalwart Druids featured large, gazing at the North Star. They were the British Druids featured in the propaganda of Julius Caesar but they were also, he suggested, Scandinavian in

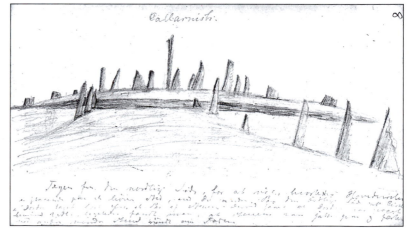
Worsaae's sketch of 1846

origin. The lively pleasures of Romance had once again triumphed over scientific enquiry. That said, in 1854 there was no idea that people could have set up such a mighty monument long before the Great Pyramid of Egypt was built.

However, Callender more than redeemed himself by including in his paper this *excellent perspective view of the structure* drawn by James Kerr, Clerk of Works to Sir James Matheson, who owned Lewis. It confirms that the peat around the circle was still intact. It adds some interesting detail. The house in the south-west part of the site (the foundations of which can still be seen today partly hidden by a corn drying kiln) was occupied, and other houses are visible to the north-west of the avenue. It seems likely that the northern part of the avenue had by then been cultivated for some time, perhaps for a century or more.

In 1857 Sir James Matheson told his chamberlain, Donald Munro, to have the stones cleared of peat. The traces of this work, completed on 2 October 1857, are still visible today, for the ground level near the stone circle is slightly lower than elsewhere. Matheson described his discoveries in a letter to the Society of Antiquaries of Scotland: *The average depth of the moss, from the surface to a rough causewayed basement in which the circle stones were imbedded, was 5 feet, and the workmen had not proceeded far with their operations, when, in front of the large central stone and extending to the eastern wing, they came upon an erection which proved, as the work proceeded, to be the walls of a chambered building, consisting of three compartments ... The larger chamber was found to have two stones on each side, forming jambs for the entrance to the smaller chamber; and in close proximity to these, there was found a separate stone, 4 feet long by 12 inches, which fitted, and was supposed to be a lintel to the jambs referred to. These stones were rough and unhewn ... I enclose some minute fragments of what we suppose to be bones found in the chamber, and a specimen of a black unctuous substance, in which these fragments were contained.*

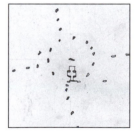

This drawing made by J Palmer, just before Sir James Matheson had the peat cleared away, shows five stones in the east row (six in fact, but the innermost is almost certainly a copying error). The extract from a neatly drawn up version of Palmer's plan, made after the clearance, includes the little chambered cairn which until then had been hidden beneath the peat. It was probably made by Captain F W L Thomas, who recorded many antiquities on the islands and who gave an illustrated talk on the stones to the Society of Antiquaries of Scotland in 1858.

Shortly after the clearance of the site, this drawing of the chamber of the cairn was made by a man called Sharbeau who had been employed by Captain Thomas. His drawing of the stone which now stands just to the south-east of the circle shows that it was lying flat in 1858. By 1867 it had been set up where it is now. Jumping ahead a little, the eastern stone of the east row was re-erected in its original socket in 1982, after excavations at the site. Thus what we see on the site today is what was buried by the peat nearly 3000 years ago, apart from missing stones in the avenue, the stone set up south-east of the circle, and, possibly, a missing stone in the western row.

In August 1885 General Pitt Rivers visited the site. He was the first Inspector of Ancient Monuments. He and his assistant, Mr Tomkins, carefully sketched and planned all the stones, noting on them the height to which they had been etched by the peat. Their work shows that even the northernmost stones of the avenue were buried 4ft deep at one time. A post card published by Valentine shows the mark on the stones quite clearly, and this delightful cartoon (based on an engraving published in 1867) has converted the colour difference between the upper and lower parts of the stones into the different colours of the clothing of 'false men'.

'Tursachan Chalanais as seen under the influence of spirits'

Lady Matheson had a path constructed from the old post office in Calanais farmhouse (it is now the Edinburgh University field centre, near to the Calanais Centre). It ran up the hill and entered the site from the south through the gate in the wall which divided Calanais farm from the township lands. It is still visible running between the stones of the south row; it originally ended at a viewing platform on the cairn inside the stone circle.

Before the clearance of the peat some of the inhabitants of Calanais had lived close to the stones, as shown in Mr Kerr's excellent perspective view (page 22). They were moved. This was a time of "improvements", affecting standing stones and people alike, and similar changes were taking place elsewhere.

The photograph here, taken in 1935, shows the stones from the south end of Calanais between the Black Houses built in the 1860s. The previous irregular spread of houses, dotted over the landscape, had been replaced by neat rows of dwellings.

Lady Matheson's path brought an intriguing variety of visitors to the stones

Although the main stone setting at Calanais was very popular with visitors to Lewis, there was little progress towards an understanding of the stones in the late nineteenth century. During the first three quarters of the twentieth century, the main site and its satellites were studied mainly by those interested in ancient astronomy. Since then there has been a renaissance during which local people have discovered many new sites.

Parts of the main setting have been excavated revealing previously hidden aspects of the site's history. Astronomy has not been forgotten, but new approaches place more emphasis on the monuments in their landscape. The stones at Calanais have inspired many modern artists; increasingly, too, it is realised that sites like those around Calanais need active conservation. These aspects of the stones are discussed in the following chapters.

5 Excavation at the main site

The excavation plan

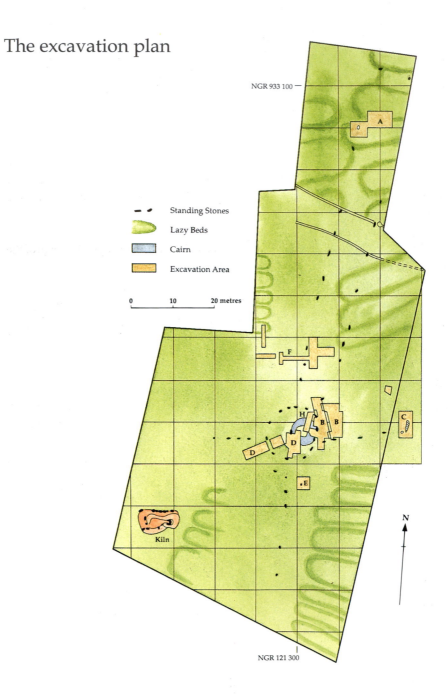

NGR 933 100 —

Standing Stones

Lazy Beds

Cairn

Excavation Area

0   10   20 metres

A

F

H
B B
D
C

D

E

N

Kiln

NGR 121 300

An over-view of the excavation

At the end of the 1970s, the chamber of the cairn was falling to bits, and visitors' feet were churning the waterlogged ground of the avenue and ring. Historic Scotland's predecessors decided that Calanais must be dug to allow repairs, and I undertook the necessary prior archaeological excavations in 1980 and 1981, with a team of helpers.

- In Area A, towards the north end of the avenue, we investigated the positions where stones were missing. We found a stone hole where MacCulloch's plan (and our survey of the electrical resistivity of the ground) suggested one might survive despite the agricultural use of this part of the site.

- Area F, half way along the west side of the avenue, had to be dug to allow drainage of the site. We found much complex detail but little illumination.

- We opened up Area C, beyond the east end of the eastern row, and retrieved a fallen stone which had been discovered by Gerald and Margaret Ponting, exactly where Palmer and others had suggested there might be one (see pages 21 and 23). We also found the stone hole in which it had originally been erected, set into ancient agricultural rigs.

- In Areas D and H we dug part of the area of the stone circle and the burial tomb. Area D contained the ditch of an ancient enclosure and more of the agricultural rigs; and its excavation showed that there were mounds of clay round the bases of the standing stones. In both Area D and H there was much evidence of the original form of the burial cairn, and of ancient acts of destruction.

- Area B, just to the east of the stone circle, contained remains of burials cleared out of the tomb in ancient times, and the foundations of a curious building.

- We dug Area E near the stone just south-east of the stone circle (discussed on page 23) to see if there was any firm evidence for a prehistoric stone hole. There was none.

Not all of our results have been analysed yet. In particular, we have been waiting for improvements in radiocarbon dating. Although dates are not yet available, the main sequence of events is fairly clear.

The early enclosure and the agricultural rigs

Imagine the land about 6000 years ago, covered by grass and scrub, and the long broad ridge rising to Cnoc an Tursa. Although rock outcropped in places, most of the ground bore soil over stiff clay. Into it, at some time during the next 800 years, people dug a small, roughly circular ditched enclosure, doubtless using antlers for picks, and shovels made of wood, or of cattle shoulder blades. It had an entrance to the north west. No trace of any structure was found inside it during excavation.

More than 5000 years ago the earth was piled up in long parallel rigs to create seed beds and to improve drainage. These rigs allowed the sun to warm the soil better, giving a few precious extra days to each growing season. The artist's impression shows people sowing barley on them. It was probably closely related to the bere still grown in the Orkney Isles, and along with animal products it formed the staple diet.

Harvesting bere in Orkney

This pottery was probably contemporary with the enclosure or the cultivation

The ring of stones

Cereal cultivation ceased, and grass and herbs grew on the rigs. Then, about 3000 BC, some kind of light structure was built in the eastern part of the area which was to be surrounded by the ring.

The stone ring was laid out. It was not a true circle. Perhaps the intention was to create a sense of direction in its layout, allowing it to face the east. Holes were dug into the stiff green clay below the soil to take the bases of the great stones, which were hauled up to the site and pushed and pulled upright. The holes were shallow, and the clay dug out of them, mixed with stones cleared from the fields, was piled round the bases of the Standing Stones to give them extra stability.

Possibly the central monolith was set up, and the south row laid out, at the same time. Some time later, another light structure was built between the eastern face of the ring and the central monolith. Many other activities doubtless took place in and around the stones.

Judging by other sites these activities may have included ritual feasts, either for the people or for their gods. Finds of henbane at a site in Fife, and fungi found on continental sites, suggest that rituals broadly of this period sometimes included drug induced hallucinations and trances. Perhaps the ring was also used during burial rituals, which may have included cremations of the dead.

Excavation inside the stone ring

Building the tomb

It is hard to estimate how many generations passed between the creation of the stone circle and building of the chambered cairn. It was long enough for a thin new soil to form, which suggests that people had used the stone ring for quite a few generations before they decided to build the tomb.

First they dug up fresh clay and spread it between the eastern face of the ring and the central monolith. Our excavation showed that the thin soil immediately under this clay overlay the mound at the base of one of the circle stones, proving that the cairn was later than the circle.

Then they laid out the chamber, with vertical slabs dividing up its interior. The lower part of its wall was vertical, but once it was a metre or so high each subsequent chamber wall-stone was laid so that it projected inward a little. The intention was to reduce the distance which had to be spanned by roof slabs. This was not strictly necessary, because the chamber was so small. The people were imitating techniques used for building larger chambers.

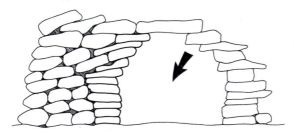

When a large chamber was needed, the builders had to stop the stones of the chamber walls from falling inward. They did this by wedging them into a supporting core cairn. The diagram to the left shows how, if people tried to build the chamber wall-face on its own, it would immediately collapse.

The small neat core cairn at Calanais was horse-shoe shaped. It rode up over the mound at the base of the central monolith, providing us with proof that the chamber was built later than the erection of that huge stone.

Excavation showed that the full extent of the cairn was completed soon afterwards. The clay under and around the core cairn had cracked in a typical polygonal pattern as the sun dried it, but it remained green and looked fresh even 5000 years later. The full cairn had a neat outer wall of horizontal slabs.

It is impossible to be sure how tall it was, because so little of it remains today, but perhaps the chamber inside it was roofed at about 1.5 metres above its floor. It was probably used for between 15 and 40 generations.

Outside the tomb passage we found scraps of pottery dating to between 2500 and 1750 BC, in black earth which we interpreted as remains of cleared-out burials. Perhaps the people believed that each person possessed multiple souls, and bodies were laid in the tomb until they decomposed, when the free spirit of the dead person could escape through the tomb passage. Once that had happened, the remains held no more power or value. The black greasy layer recorded by Matheson in 1857 (as described on page 22) may have been the residue of decomposition.

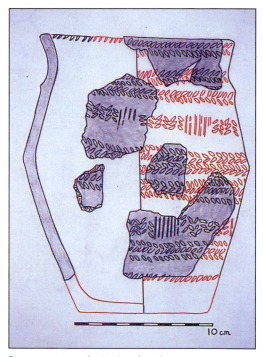

Reconstruction of a beaker found during excavation

10 cm

Quartz and Skye mylonite arrowheads found during excavation

The avenue and the rows of stones

Cnoc an Tursa

The fallen stone revealed

The stone in it's socket

Excavation provided some important information about the avenue and rows. It is unlikely that they originally crossed the circle, because no suitable stone holes were found inside it. Some early descriptions were shown to be accurate. There was a stone hole near the north end of the west side of the avenue where MacCulloch had shown a fallen stone on his plan in 1819. That means there were probably 5 stones in each of the west, south and east rows, and 16 or so on each side of the avenue – perhaps even 19, as Martin Martin claimed in 1703. However, recent excavation by Edinburgh University on the other side of the wall at the south end of the site has revealed remains of several pits, and it is possible that there were either more stones in the south row or a structure of some kind between it and the natural rock outcrop, Cnoc an Tursa.

By 1980 it had long been suspected that there was still a fallen stone at the east end of the east row, beyond the edge of the area in the care of the state. Shortly before our excavations Gerald and Margaret Ponting carefully probed the peat and located it precisely.

We located the stone hole through excavation. When we set the stone up again it fitted exactly into its socket. It is thus precisely where it originally stood, and the orientation of its faces is as it was.

It was important to try to discover when the avenue and the rows were built. People have suggested that they were designed to indicate the rising and setting of the sun, the moon and the bright star Capella, which is part of the constellation of the Charioteer, on the edge of the Milky Way. Since the direction in which the earth's north pole points at the heavens changes gradually over the centuries, the points on the horizon at which heavenly bodies rise or set changes with time. Alas, no new dating evidence was found.

Judging by other sites, alignments of stones were built from 3000 BC to 1000 BC. There is an increasing suspicion that some of them started short and had stones added to them. That might explain the change in direction of the west side of the avenue. There remains plenty of potential for evidence where we did not dig – that is one reason for conserving Calanais very carefully.

Rejecting the ancestors

At some time in the second millennium BC the cairn became dilapidated, or was purposefully despoiled. The area inside the ring was harrowed, probably with a single pronged harrow which left grooves in the ground (there were similar marks just outside the ring). In the soil were many charcoal and pottery fragments. This may have been ordinary agriculture, but it seems more likely that the people despoiled the cairn and harrowed the site to make absolutely sure that no inconvenient ancestors would come back to trouble them – a ritual cleansing.

The climate was variable throughout the second millennium BC, and it became cooler and wetter as the centuries drew on. At some time a small structure was built just east of the ring. Its back was formed by the edge of the cairn, where slabs (probably roofing slabs from the passage or chamber) were set up vertically. Perhaps the curving wall which formed the north side of the structure was built up in turf on the stone foundation, and perhaps it had a roof; but alas, no evidence survived.

The whole site was probably abandoned about 800 BC (give or take a century or two) because that is when, helped by colder, wetter conditions, blanket peat started to form around it.

6 Modern ideas and ancient astronomy

That strange activity, standing stones on their ends in the earth, may have had many meanings and motives. Perhaps free land was becoming scarce as populations grew, and the communities controlled the resulting stress through ceremony. Maybe the rising sea, its daily surge governed by the moon, had to be controlled by ritual and magic. Possibly restless individuals saw a way of imposing their wills on others in the name of some strong new belief. From whatever deep well their inspiration rose, people seem to have given material expression to beliefs about the sun and the moon at Calanais, as they did at the huge burial tombs of Maes Howe in Orkney and New Grange in Ireland.

The changes in the position of sunrise and sunset vary regularly over the year

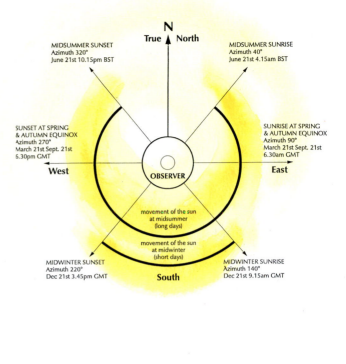

MIDSUMMER SUNSET
Azimuth 320°
June 21st 10.15pm BST

True North
N

MIDSUMMER SUNRISE
Azimuth 40°
June 21st 4.15am BST

SUNSET AT SPRING
& AUTUMN EQUINOX
Azimuth 270°
March 21st Sept. 21st
6.30pm GMT

SUNRISE AT SPRING
& AUTUMN EQUINOX
Azimuth 90°
March 21st Sept. 21st
6.30am GMT

West

OBSERVER

East

movement of the sun
at midsummer
(long days)

movement of the sun
at midwinter
(short days)

MIDWINTER SUNSET
Azimuth 220°
Dec 21st 3.45pm GMT

South

MIDWINTER SUNRISE
Azimuth 140°
Dec 21st 9.15am GMT

The sun, the moon and the bright stars are very obvious to those who live without artificial light. The sun searches north till midsummer's day, and then flees south for winter. The moon wheels through its companionable cycles, reflecting sun and earthshine.

In the latitude of Calanais the path of the sun varies greatly from summer to winter. The extreme settings of the moon are more complicated; they change over an 18.6 year period, as does the moon's greatest height in the southern skies. Wider changes take place over periods measured in tens of thousands of years. Indeed, the pattern of the sky is new every time the seasons return, though the differences from year to year are subtle. Various modern authors have contended that the rows of stones at Calanais indicated precise setting points of heavenly bodies at particular times in the past.

The moon orbits the earth about 13 times a year. During each lunar month moonrise and moon-set swing from most northerly to most southerly positions and back again. Because the moon's orbit is slightly tilted, the difference between most northerly and most southerly positions varies regularly over a period of 18.61 years. The diagram shows the extremes, 9.305 years apart (at the end of a full cycle the positions return to where they started).

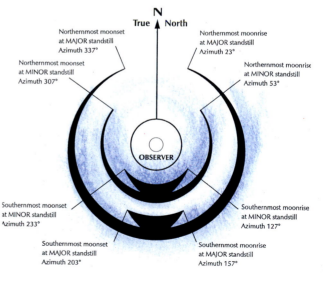

N
True North

Northernmost moonset
at MAJOR standstill
Azimuth 337°

Northernmost moonrise
at MAJOR standstill
Azimuth 23°

Northernmost moonset
at MINOR standstill
Azimuth 307°

Northernmost moonrise
at MINOR standstill
Azimuth 53°

OBSERVER

Southernmost moonset
at MINOR standstill
Azimuth 233°

Southernmost moonrise
at MINOR standstill
Azimuth 127°

Southernmost moonset
at MAJOR standstill
Azimuth 203°

Southernmost moonrise
at MAJOR standstill
Azimuth 157°

To the doyen of twentieth century archaeo-astronomy, Alexander Thom, it was more likely than not that astronomical observations were built into the patterns of the stones. He believed that stone settings were set out using a precise measure, which he called the megalithic yard. He tried to show that the directions indicated by drawing lines between stones proved the existence of a prehistoric calendar.

In studies typified by accurate surveys, a careful choice of sites and statistical expertise, Clive Ruggles has shown that claims of precise alignments are not securely founded. The alignments thought to be significant are few enough that they may have occurred by chance. Absence of evidence is, of course, not evidence of absence: his trial of the facts has ended in that uncomfortably honest Scottish verdict, Not Proven.

Yet there is an abiding fascination in the relationship between ancient stone settings, the land and the sky. Amongst many farming peoples the yearly round is divided up by ritual activities, such as festivals. Their timing is made regular by astronomical observations.

There are signs that society became more stratified around 3000 BC; that the differences between leaders and the led became stronger. The ability to say when ceremonies should occur may have stimulated this process, or it may have been a by-product of it. Modern studies have focussed on the relationships between stone settings, the landscape and the rising and setting of heavenly bodies.

The time and place, of moon-set, for instance, depends on the height of the horizon. Margaret and Ron Curtis, of Calanais, have drawn accurate profiles of the horizons as seen from the stones, and have recorded the directions indicated by looking between various sites. It is clear that the design of the main site, at least, incorporated a remarkable relationship between the landscape and the heavens. Every 18.6 years, viewed from the avenue, the moon dances low over the hills to the south, sets, and then gleams bright within the silhouette of the stone circle as it passes a notch in the horizon.

The landscape, looking to the south from Cnoc an Tursa, illustrates a modern interpretation of this sort of belief system. Some have seen a "sleeping beauty" in the profile of the hills, where the moon dances low every 18.6 years. In this interpretation, people relate the movements of the heavenly bodies to the landscape as a whole. The Gaelic for this profile, "Cailleach na mòintich" (The old woman of the moors) reflects an older tradition.

Past perceptions and modern understandings

Archaeology tells us something about how people lived, but it does not tell us what they felt, nor what they thought. We seek to understand their ideas through analogies with better known societies, assuming that tools and buildings reflect the beliefs of those who fashioned them; but present perceptions of past peoples are not the same as past peoples' perceptions of their own present. That said, archaeology provides no evidence that we have changed much during the last ten thousand years. In many societies, animals, plants, objects and natural phenomena are thought to contain spirits, while people themselves have multiple souls, which do not all depart this world at death. A place in society can be gained by asserting power over these spiritual entities.

These general ideas are supported by the evidence from Calanais, and at sites like Maes Howe and New Grange. It does seem, beyond reasonable doubt, that the layout of some tombs and stone settings took account of astronomical events.

However no techniques so far devised have proved that alignments were, in a modern sense, precise. There is a need to devise new ways to assess the relationships between ancient structures in their landscape, ancient beliefs and ancient astronomy.

Although, so far, we have not been able to reincarnate ancient truths, the stones allow a different set of modern insights and interpretations. In the next chapter we shall see how they illuminate the present.

7 Illuminating the stones

Sarah at the Stones. Sam Maynard, 1989

Does it matter what artists and poets say about Calanais, if they build their art on scraps of eighteenth century ideas about a nobler past, and twentieth century fantasies of idyllic climates and benign astronomer-priests? Does it matter if they project modern wickedness onto ancient stones through nineteenth century notions of druids?

Those who set up the stones, their true motives hidden behind the silent mask of time; those who shut dead bodies and live spirits in the tomb; the farmers who ploughed among the stones; Victorian romantics cloistered a sea and a country away; modern archaeo-astronomers, ley-line hunters, archaeologists and artists and poets, like those whose works figure here, have created a subtle threading of objects and ideas which is the real and ever growing Calanais.

Halloween. 53 x 80 cms. Eric Hoffmann, 1985

The stones of Calanais may stand another five thousand years. Then our descendants will look back, and we shall be part of their history. They will talk of the Stones' creation and use, and of what we do now, as things nearly equal in importance, for there is a very human richness and diversity both in the activities which took place at Calanais between 5000 and 3000 years ago, and in people's responses to the stones today.

Alignment Receiver-Calanais. Sculpture of painted wood and bronze, 77 x 35 x 20 cms. Will Maclean, 1995

Callanish. Etching/mezzotint, 50 x 33 cms. Reinhard Behrens, 1980

> "It is left by traditione that these were a sort of men converted into stone by ane Inchanter"

John Morisone of South Bragar
c. 1684

The March of the Standing Stones, Edinburgh Festival Fringe.
George Wyllie, 1985 (Photograph Marius Alexander)

At the Stones of Callanish

At the Stones of Callanish yesterday I heard one woman saying to another: 'This is where they burnt the children in early times.' I did not see druids among the planets nor sun nor robe: but I saw a beautiful blue ball like heaven cracking and children with skin hanging to them like the flag in which Nagasaki was sacrificed.

Iain Crichton Smith.

(Iain Crichton Smith, Collected Poems, 1992 Carcanet Press).

At Callanish Stones

The circle had neither end nor beginning,
our thought had neither start nor finish,
the still universe was waiting,
sea not stroking the land,
grass not moving in wind,
there was no day, no night —
and I shall never forget
your fair hair and tender lips,
or the shared desire that wove us
together in time's circle
where treachery will not touch hope's shore.

Derick Thomson.

(Derick Thomson, Creachadh na Clàrsaich, 1982 Macdonald Publishers).

Reagan at Callanish. Murdo MacLeod, 1985

Young boy with rising moon, Callanish, Isle of Lewis. Gus Wylie, 1985

8 Conservation

The raising of the stone

Conservation of the site has been necessary ever since it was cleared of peat. The stone immediately south-east of the ring was erected before 1867, and Lady Matheson had a path constructed from the south gate of the site to the ring. For some of its length it was raised up above the surrounding ground, probably because the ground was waterlogged. Routine maintenance was carried out: during excavations we found layers of what we called 'Ministry grit', after the Ministry of Works, no doubt the residues of attempts to repair erosion.

During the 1970s the number of visitors increased, and their feet churned up the often waterlogged ground. This damaged the vegetation, destroyed archaeological evidence and made Calanais unsightly. Some visitors could not resist climbing the stones and racing around and over the tomb; it began to fall to bits. In 1980 and 1981 the ground and the tomb were repaired, and drains were inserted, after archaeological investigation to ensure that little information would be destroyed without record.

It was important to ensure that all proactive conservation was well justified. The stone at the east end of the eastern row could be re-erected because there was an exact match between the original packing stones in the hole and the base of the stone, and because antiquarian accounts showed that the stone fell only recently. On the other hand, although there was no positive evidence that the small stone south-east of the circle was in a prehistoric position, that absence of evidence was inadequate to allow removal.

Since then visitor pressure on the site has not decreased. It has become necessary to persuade tourists to stay at the edges of the site. A path has been laid on terram matting (so it can be removed cleanly) just inside the fence, and notices request visitors to respect the fragility of the ground surface.

The new Calanais Centre is a still more positive approach to balancing the needs of the site, the community and visitors. It includes a display about the sites of the Calanais area. Visitors can learn about the main site without damaging it; yet they are free to walk among the Stones.

The link between the Stones, the land and the people living around Loch Roag is 5000 years old. The Centre, run by the local trust Urras nan Tursachan, hopes to strengthen pride in the deep past of the Western Isles. It is situated next door to the Edinburgh University field centre, which serves as a base for investigations of the surrounding area. Thus conservation and display of the Standing Stones is part of a wider effort to heighten understanding of the fragile heritage left to us by our ancestors.

Further reading

The fullest descriptions of previous accounts of Calanais are practically unobtainable except, with luck, through libraries. Gerald and Margaret Ponting's **Callanish, the documentary record** (volume 1 on the main site and volume 2 on the satellite sites) is indispensable to those with a serious interest in the stones; republication is long overdue. My own 'Callanish' in **Studies in Scottish Antiquity** (John Donald 1983) edited by David Breeze is hardly more readily available.

The sites on the map and in the table at the beginning of Chapter 3 are shown in more detail, with large scale plans, on a map leaflet published by Glasgow University Department of Geography.

The best single source of detailed information on the earlier part of Britain's prehistory, including descriptions of sites and artefacts, is probably still J V S Megaw and D D A Simpson's **Introduction to British prehistory**, published by Leicester University Press in 1979. It provides a solid foundation for accounts of more recent discoveries. Also **Scotland: Archaeology and early history**, by Graham and Anna Ritchie (Thames and Hudson 1981) is a sound and accessible source book.

Audrey Henshall's **Chambered Tombs of Scotland** published by Edinburgh University Press in two volumes, one in 1963 and the other in 1972, is the most authoritative account of burial places like the small chambered tomb in the stone ring at Calanais.

Aubrey Burl, through Yale University Press, has published two informative and vigorously written accounts of stone settings. **The Stone Circles of the British Isles** (1976) is still the best general account of Scotland's rich heritage of stone circles although, because it was published before Calanais was excavated, its account of Calanais is out of date. His **From Carnac to Callanish** published in 1994, describes avenues, stone rows and alignment.

By far the best book on artefacts like those found at Calanais is **Symbols of Power at the Time of Stonehenge**, by D V Clarke, T G Cowie and A Fox. It was published by HMSO, and its superb illustrations and intriguing text appeal to both specialists and amateurs of archaeology.

Two recent books give rich accounts of the environmental background: **Late Quaternary Environmental Change**, published by Longman in 1992 and written by Martin Bell and Michael Walker gives a wealth of information, as does the somewhat more technical **Climate Change and Human Impact on the Landscape**, edited by F M Chambers and published in paperback by Chapman and Hall in 1993.

The series **Exploring Scotland's Heritage**, published by HMSO for the Royal Commission on the Ancient and Historical Monuments of Scotland provides a good account of accessible sites of all periods, including excursion itineraries. The volume on Argyll and the Western Isles by Graham Ritchie and Mary Harman is worth reading for islanders and tourists alike.

Historic Scotland, through HMSO, has published several good general accounts of Scotland's past, concentrating on sites which can still be visited. **Scotland BC,** by Anna Ritchie is particularly relevant.

Historic Scotland has also entered into a partnership with B T Batsford Limited to produce accessible accounts of Scotland's past. **Scotland's First Settlers** by Caroline Wickham Jones, published in 1994, is about Scotland's hunter-gatherers in the times before the stones were set up at Calanais. My own **Ancient Scotland**, to be published in 1996, will concentrate on explaining Scotland's past in terms of those tombs, stone settings, enclosures, artefacts, settlements and field systems which have been dated by the radiocarbon technique, in an attempt to provide a counterbalance to the weaknesses of traditional archaeological dating.